Love Making EXPERIENCES

VICTORIA KIRBY

I0400271

Copyright © 2019 by Victoria Kirby.

ISBN Softcover 978-1-950580-03-3

All rights reserved. No part of this book may be reproduced or transmitted in any form or by any means, electronic or mechanical, including photocopying, recording, or by any information storage and retrieval system without express written permission from the author, except in the case of brief quotations embodied in critical reviews and certain other non-commercial uses permitted by copyright law.

Printed in the United States of America.

To order additional copies of this book, contact:
Bookwhip
1-855-339-3589
https://www.bookwhip.com

Dedication

This journal is dedicated to those who can take a look back into their past and doesn't allow it to affect their future. Who can just look at certain situations as a lesson learnt?

Preface

Sometimes in life as people we walk on a straight and narrow path. Sure, along the way some of us face a few roadblocks. But, it's how you face those few roadblocks which can make you the type of person that you are. Furthermore, the majority of both female and male couples are loyal to each other. But, we must also remember that some men and women both have wondering eyes. As in to say it doesn't hurt to look. But, we must also remember some men and women both have their insecurities.

Question Starters

1. Who was the best/worst you've ever had?
2. Did you meet on a dating site?
3. Did you wear any protection or have raw sex?
4. Did you do any role playing?
5. Would you ever double back to an ex?
6. Did you ever teach a man or woman how to make love to you?
7. Would you ever tell your parents or best friend about your sex life?
8. Has any man ever made love to you so good that you came on your menstrual cycle?
9. Would you ever invite a third person into your bedroom?
10. Do you find that music gets you into the mood?

Top 5 T.O.T.D.

- Always feel and look attractive to your mate to keep the spark going
- Never invite a third party into your bedroom
- Use a few props once in a while to keep your mate happy
- Try not to have sex while you're sick with the flu or a cold
- Keep a calendar to remind you of the important dates

Self-Reminder

If as humans we always remind ourselves that we deserve someone who's going to love us as their equal, then everyone will know their true worth. But, if either female or male don't know their true worth they might be bound to be depressed at times. Though, a person who's depressed has gone through a little heartache and pain. Furthermore, a good conversation never hurts anyone long as it doesn't go too far. Then again, some people would rather Netflix and chill by themselves.

JANUARY

Mo	Tu	We	Th	Fr	Sa	Su
	1	2	3	4	5	6
7	8	9	10	11	12	13
14	15	16	17	18	19	20
21	22	23	24	25	26	27
28	29	30	31			

FEBRUARY

Mo	Tu	We	Th	Fr	Sa	Su
				1	2	3
4	5	6	7	8	9	10
11	12	13	14	15	16	17
18	19	20	21	22	23	24
25	26	27	28			

MARCH

Mo	Tu	We	Th	Fr	Sa	Su
				1	2	3
4	5	6	7	8	9	10
11	12	13	14	15	16	17
18	19	20	21	22	23	24
25	26	27	28	29	30	31

APRIL

Mo	Tu	We	Th	Fr	Sa	Su
1	2	3	4	5	6	7
8	9	10	11	12	13	14
15	16	17	18	19	20	21
22	23	24	25	26	27	28
29	30					

MAY

Mo	Tu	We	Th	Fr	Sa	Su
		1	2	3	4	5
6	7	8	9	10	11	12
13	14	15	16	17	18	19
20	21	22	23	24	25	26
27	28	29	30	31		

JUNE

Mo	Tu	We	Th	Fr	Sa	Su
					1	2
3	4	5	6	7	8	9
10	11	12	13	14	15	16
17	18	19	20	21	22	23
24	25	26	27	28	29	30

JULY

Mo	Tu	We	Th	Fr	Sa	Su
1	2	3	4	5	6	7
8	9	10	11	12	13	14
15	16	17	18	19	20	21
22	23	24	25	26	27	28
29	30	31				

AUGUST

Mo	Tu	We	Th	Fr	Sa	Su
			1	2	3	4
5	6	7	8	9	10	11
12	13	14	15	16	17	18
19	20	21	22	23	24	25
26	27	28	29	30	31	

SEPTEMBER

Mo	Tu	We	Th	Fr	Sa	Su
						1
2	3	4	5	6	7	8
9	10	11	12	13	14	15
16	17	18	19	20	21	22
23	24	25	26	27	28	29
30						

OCTOBER

Mo	Tu	We	Th	Fr	Sa	Su
	1	2	3	4	5	6
7	8	9	10	11	12	13
14	15	16	17	18	19	20
21	22	23	24	25	26	27
28	29	30	31			

NOVEMBER

Mo	Tu	We	Th	Fr	Sa	Su
				1	2	3
4	5	6	7	8	9	10
11	12	13	14	15	16	17
18	19	20	21	22	23	24
25	26	27	28	29	30	

DECEMBER

Mo	Tu	We	Th	Fr	Sa	Su
						1
2	3	4	5	6	7	8
9	10	11	12	13	14	15
16	17	18	19	20	21	22
23	24	25	26	27	28	29
30	31					

Dear Readers

Always remember that there's a writer within everyone. It's just that sometimes everyone who has a story to tell doesn't know exactly how to start it off. But, then again writing is a talent that some people inherit while others inherit other talents. Some people better express themselves on paper verses having a full conversation with another person. For example, with most people I would rather text them or write it down verses having a conversation. Most people words run together while when you write it down you have to think before you speak. All in all, everyone who has a talent and those who haven't quite discovered what their talent is it's just best to use it wisely. Good talent shouldn't have to go to waste. Always remember that most people talent makes them money. And who would really want to let good legit money go to waste?

www.ingramcontent.com/pod-product-compliance
Lightning Source LLC
Chambersburg PA
CBHW030135100526
44591CB00009B/671
9781950580033